Ariana Madix

famously discovered her partner was unfaithful, and the incident—known as Scandoval—captivated audiences worldwide. She has now reclaimed her power, channeling her pain into a resounding statement of strength and resilience in *Single AF Cocktails*, a collection of alluring drinks that follows the trajectory of a relationship that starts beautifully but ends in disaster.

The newly solo Ariana serves up her own recipes and perspective in a unique exploration of the stages of a doomed relationship. In her own words, Ariana takes back the narrative of her very public breakup while inspiring others to find inner strength in their own troubles. Each drink tells part of the story from her point of view, from when she first met her ex, through the insidious affair and its painful aftermath, and to her present state, coming out the other side, stronger than before.

Cleverly categorized into relationship-inspired sections—Honeymoon Phase, Betrayal, Devastation, Resilience, and Ad Astra—*Single AF Cocktails* offers a range of boozy concoctions for whatever your mood, from when you feel like burning it all down to when it's time to rally your ride-or-die squad. You'll find recipes like Rumors, with dark crème de cassis that floats on top of the drink before bleeding into the spirits below, the way lies may find their way into your relationship, or We Ride at Dawn, a bold mezcal margarita that's equal parts power and healing.

Full of stunning photography and never-before-told stories, *Single AF Cocktails* is a singular experience for the reader as they ride the rollercoaster of Ariana's story alongside her. Whether you're a longtime fan or a newcomer to Ariana's world, *Single AF Cocktails* promises a captivating and cathartic experience for all.

Single AF Cocktails

Single AF Cocktails

Drinks for
Bad B*tches

Ariana

tails
a Madix

Photographs by
Kelly Puleio

Clarkson
Potter/
Publishers
New York

Library of Congress Control Number: 2023940908

ISBN: 978-0-593-79687-0
Ebook ISBN: 978-0-593-79688-7

Printed in the United States of America

Photography: Kelly Puleio
Photo shoot art direction: Kelly Puleio and Maxwell Newton
Photo shoot producer: Tamara Costa
Photo assistant and lighting: Katja Bresch
Cocktail styling: Trevin Hutchins
Cocktail assistant: Lena Conley
Prop stylist: Maxwell Newton
Prop assistants: Cory Fisher and Brandon Loyd
Photo shoot production assistant: Wendy Helie

Editor: Jennifer Sit | Editorial assistant: Bianca Cruz
Art Director: Stephanie Huntwork
Designer: Laura Palese
Production editor: Mark McCauslin
Production manager: Phil Leung
Compositor: Merri Ann Morrell
Copyeditor: Carole Berglie
Proofreaders: Jacob Sammon and Nicole Celli
Publicists: Erica Gelbard and Jana Branson
Marketers: Allison Renzulli and Chloe Aryeh

First Edition

CONTENTS

Introduction

I'm not the first woman to be betrayed by a person she loves, and I certainly won't be the last.

IF you've picked up this book, you might already know the story of what happened between me and my ex, Tom Sandoval, because most of it played out on the Bravo show *Vanderpump Rules* in early 2023. Tom and I were together for 9 years (like 56 years in dog years) before he had an affair with our co-star (and my friend at the time) Raquel Leviss. The media dubbed the event #Scandoval.

Having the whole thing unfold publicly was painful. Everyone had their own hot take on all of the people involved, and it's easy to lose sight of what is real and what isn't when you're in the middle of a storm of rumors and sensational headlines. I've had a lot of people support me throughout this time, and a lot of people treat me like a villain, or worse: like I deserved the betrayal that I was served.

Taking inspiration from classic albums about betrayal like Alanis Morissette's *Jagged Little Pill,* Kacey Musgraves' *Star-Crossed,* and Beyoncé's *Lemonade,* I wrote this book as a way of reclaiming the narrative—of channeling my pain into something creative instead of destructive.

I've been bartending since 2008, so making drinks has always been in my wheelhouse. When Tom and I were on the show together, it was also something that we did together—it's how we met, and the reason why we wrote our first book, *Fancy AF Cocktails.* It was something people associated with our relationship, but bartending has always, and will always, remain my thing. That's why my "breakup album" is a book of cocktail recipes. This is me planting my flag in the ground, proving that I don't have to give up a part of myself just because we are no longer together.

Getting betrayed is a universal experience—many of us have been there—so I wanted to share my side of the story through cocktails because I hope it helps others who are going through the same thing. During this time, I have seen such an outpouring of support that it has felt surreal and even overwhelming in moments. But more than anything, it has given me hope, and my wish is that if you relate to my story on a personal level, it makes you feel less alone, too.

In this book, you'll find sixty cocktail recipes that follow the trajectory of a relationship that starts beautifully but ends in disaster. Each drink tells part of the story of what happened from my perspective—from when we first met, through the affair and its aftermath, to now as I am coming out the other side. These stories are all very real and very personal, written during an emotionally raw time in my life.

From the early days of getting to know each other better and traveling around the world (High Down Under, page 37) to our first home (Together Forever, page 44), the first chapter details my honeyed memories of the good times in our relationship. The middle two chapters—Betrayal and Devastation—recount the heart-wrenching moments that defined his infidelity, like when I found out about the affair (Explosion, page 73), and how strange it's been to reflect on the events of the past year knowing he was sneaking around behind my back the entire time (Double Life, page 96). The final two chapters, Resilience and Ad Astra, tell the stories of when my family and friends rallied behind me (Support System, page 118) and of my journey back to feeling like an independent woman with renewed hope for the future (What Doesn't Kill Me, page 146).

You can read the recipe headnotes from the beginning of the book to the end if you want the whole story, or if you're just here for the cocktails, you can skip around to pick out a drink that best matches your situation. There are a lot of bomb-ass cocktail recipes to enjoy, and that is reason enough to dig in. In the back, you'll find an index of all of the cocktails organized by base spirit or category, so you can quickly turn to a vodka or whiskey drink, for example. Most of these recipes are created for one—there's no shame in enjoying a glass of sangria on your own after work—but if you want to scale up for a crowd, simply multiply the ingredient quantities by the number of people you are serving.

I hope you get something out of it all. Maybe my story will help you see red flags in your own relationship, or point out areas for personal growth, or encourage you to find your own voice in the wake of a bad breakup.

More than anything, going through this situation and writing this book have reminded me of the work I need to keep doing on myself. Although I was so hurt by the affair, the truth is that he has his own wonderful qualities and I have my own toxic traits too. I am fiercely loyal and trusting but am also impatient at times. I get in my own head constantly—always fearing that I am never enough. I'm quick to snap at people when I'm anxious, and I care too much about what people think. I can sometimes be frozen in my own state of depression if I'm down. Learning to love yourself is a process, one that's so important for me to continue.

On a larger note, my goal is that this book shows that we can let go of the shame and embarrassment that can happen in these situations. I am not ashamed. I am not embarrassed. I believe everyone has the right to feel comfortable talking about these kinds of issues, even if it's just with friends over drinks. Maybe this book will be a part of making that a reality.

When you get to the end, hopefully you feel the same way I did after going through this process: like I've closed the door on this chapter in my life, and I can move on. Let's raise a glass to that—to all of the badass bitches coming out of horrible breakups stronger than before. We are all better off for it! ●

Tools

Every home bar needs a good tool kit in order to make cocktails like the pros. Here are the basics.

Shaker: There are several kinds of shakers you can use to make cocktails, but I prefer the Boston-style shaker—the kind with a metal shaking tin and glass mixing tin—because they are easy to clean. You can also see the liquids go into the glass side in real time, to make sure you haven't forgotten any ingredients as you build the drink, which is helpful.

Muddler: Muddlers come in all shapes and sizes, but I like the ones with the teeth on the bottom, which help break up big chunks of fruit better than ones with no teeth. For best results, find a muddler that best fits the size and shape of your hand.

Strainer: Hawthorne strainers are the most common type—they have stainless steel wire that makes the strainer fit snugly within the mixing tin and helps catch all the little bits of fruit you don't want in the drink. Some people use a julep strainer for straining stirred drinks, but you can use a Hawthorne strainer for that as well, so you don't need to double up, unless you want to.

Bar spoons: Heavier bar spoons make it easier to stir, so find a nice long one that has a relatively good weight on the spoon end.

Jigger: Measuring liquid amounts is key to making drinks that taste good, so always use a jigger. The best ones are those that list common pour measurements on the inside or outside of the jigger, so you need only one for every amount, instead of having to buy three different sizes.

Ice molds: Back when I first started bartending, there weren't many options for at-home ice molds, but ice has never been hotter than it is today, so you can find a ton of great options, from small 1-inch cubes to large single spheres. There are also molds that come in fun shapes like flowers or puppies or skulls, so you can really personalize your ice. Just be sure to pick ones made of silicone—the ones with a lid are best because they prevent freezer burn.

Glassware

Specialty glassware from places like CB2, Cocktail Kingdom, and other online retailers gives you the chance to add some personal flair to your drinks. Aside from those, which are great for special occasions, I recommend always having a set of basics on hand so you can accommodate whatever drinking occasions arise.

Standard rocks: Use for drinks like the old fashioned, or margarita on the rocks. Make sure it's large enough to hold 7 to 12 ounces of liquid, so there is enough room for plenty of ice, or in case you are in the mood for a double.

Collins: For drinks that include soda, like highballs, find a tall, skinny Collins glass. The best Collins glasses hold about 12 ounces of liquid, with enough room to add a generous stack of ice cubes.

Shot: Everyone needs a good collection of shot glasses for times when only shots will do. Stock enough for a big group of friends—there is nothing worse than having to give someone a shot in a plastic cup when everyone else gets the good glass ones.

Coupe: The curvy coupe glass has come back into popularity with a vengeance during the last decade. They are so pretty and add a really elegant feel to classy cocktails like the martini and Manhattan.

Martini: An old reliable standby, the V-shaped martini glass has never gone out of style. You can use this for classic cocktails and modern martinis, too.

Champagne flute: Tall and slender, these glasses have a stem so your hand doesn't warm your drink. They are designed for Champagne, of course, and for any cocktail that features sparkling wine, such as a mimosa.

Hurricane: This glass is tall with a stem and an undulating fluted shape, perfect for fruity, tropical drinks like a Singapore sling or piña colada.

The Dos & Don'ts of Drink Mixing

Do

● Use a jigger to measure the ingredients to make sure the cocktail doesn't taste too strong or too sweet.

● Shake the shit out of the drink! A half-hearted, limp-wristed shake won't get all the ingredients to blend together correctly. Really put your back into it.

● Chill your glassware while you are making the cocktail; this ensures the drink will stay colder for a longer period of time. Plus, the pretty frost that shows up after pulling a chilled glass from the freezer screams elegance.

● Make each drink your own. Substitute a spirit or liqueur if you prefer tequila instead of gin, or have an allergy to mango or basil, for example. If you don't like it, you can always make another one. Have fun with it!

● Embrace the mocktail. There have never been more delicious options for alcohol-free drinks, which are great for when you are not drinking, and there is no shame in skipping the booze every once in a while.

Don't

● Don't add more booze than the recipe calls for—doing so will make the cocktail taste less than fabulous. If you want more booze, have a shot on the side!

● Don't skimp on the ice, especially when it comes to shaking. When you don't have enough ice in the tin, the cocktail will come out lukewarm and gross.

● Don't use sour mix when you can use fresh-squeezed lemon or lime juice. The difference in flavor is like night and day.

● Don't leave vermouth on the shelf; it is wine-based and will start to oxidize when left out at room temperature.

● Don't forget to taste test your drink before serving it to friends, to make sure it is the best version of that drink it can be. Taste with a straw and then throw the straw away.

LINE
of events

EYMOON

PHASE

those shimmering days

In the TRENCHES

A BEAUTIFUL but
Chaotic Martini

Serves 1 Looking back at the beginnings of a relationship, your memories can have this perfect, crystalline quality to them, and the drink that embodies those feelings for me is the iconic Vesper Martini. When I moved to Los Angeles, I got a job as a bartender at Lisa Vanderpump's restaurant Villa Blanca, in Beverly Hills. That was where I first met him. Right from the beginning, we worked really well together because we both brought something different to the table: He was really great with customers, so he would cover the floor; I was less interested in chatting with the Beverly Hills crowd and more into keeping my head down and getting the cocktails mixed, so I covered the service well.

When you're working with other people in a bar, you're in the trenches together, so bonding happens really quickly. We were both in relationships with other people at the time, but we would swap advice and support each other whenever things got rough. We quickly became friends that way.

We made a lot of martinis there—shaken, not stirred, the way James Bond ordered them—so this cocktail is an elegant but bold Vesper Martini, an homage to the way our relationship began in such a beautiful but chaotic environment.

1½ oz.	gin
½ oz.	vodka
½ oz.	Lillet Blanc apéritif
1 to 2 dashes	orange bitters
	Ice cubes
	Lemon twist, to garnish

Combine the gin, vodka, Lillet, and orange bitters in a mixing glass ● Add ice and stir to chill ● Strain into a martini glass and garnish with a lemon twist ●

Good
CHEMISTRY
A SPICY *Margarita*

	Lime wedge
	Kosher salt, to rim the glass
3	slices of jalapeño, 2 to muddle and 1 to garnish
¾ oz.	agave nectar
¾ oz.	Nixta Licor de Elote (see Note)
1 oz.	fresh lime juice
1 oz.	mezcal
1 oz.	tequila
	Ice cubes

Serves 1 Good chemistry and a bit of heat—what could go wrong? When I first joined *Vanderpump Rules*, people immediately began to speculate about our relationship, because we were friends before I joined the cast. I think a lot of people saw our natural chemistry, even before we did.

When it comes to cocktails, I love the alchemy that happens between hot chiles and agave spirits, so this is a spicy margarita made with both tequila and mezcal—the smoke from the latter deepens the flavors of the former in a way I adore.

NOTE ● Nixta is a super cool Mexican corn liqueur with a soft sweetness that plays well off the smoke of the mezcal and spice of the jalapeño. But you could also use your favorite orange liqueur instead, if you prefer.

Prepare your rocks glass by running a lime wedge across half the rim and dipping the rim in salt ● Muddle two of the jalapeños with the agave nectar and Nixta in a shaker tin ● Add the lime juice, mezcal, and tequila, then add ice ● Shake to combine ● Strain into a rocks glass, add a few ice cubes, and garnish with the remaining jalapeño ●

At My SIDE

A comforting COGNAC OLD FASHIONED

Serves 1 The feeling of warmth and comfort from a partner or friend can be like no other, and this cocktail captures that, like a hug in a glass. It tastes almost like banana bread, with its high-quality banana liqueur and warm vanilla-like Cognac.

The night my dad passed away, I was at Scheana's apartment because I was coming out of a bad relationship and needed some time with my besties. I remember getting the call with the news and having a full-on meltdown. Scheana called him and told him what was going on, and he dropped everything to come be there at my side. He sat with me the whole night while I cried. In that moment, he really showed what a good friend he could be, and this drink brings me back to that place.

NOTE ● Measure precisely because the quality of this drink really hinges on exact measurements.

2 oz.	Cognac
½ oz.	Tempus Fugit crème de banane
1 dash	Angostura bitters
	Ice cubes

In a mixing glass, combine the Cognac, liqueur, and bitters ● Add ice and stir at a leisurely pace to chill ● Strain into a rocks glass, and add a single large ice cube ● Cozy up on your favorite couch and sip this drink slowly to savor every warming drop ●

CHARLOTTE

BOUNTIFUL BERRIES and *Botanicals*

Serves 1 I adopted Charlotte from the Humane Society in St. Augustine when I was going to Flagler College. She was my soul dog—the most beautiful girl, with lovely blond fur and a pink-ish tail. She might have been small in size, but she was my dire wolf. My best friend. My soul mate. We had the most intense connection that I think every dog owner can understand. I had to say goodbye to her last summer, and I still miss her every day. Charlotte is in the clouds now; so in homage to her sweet spirit, this cocktail features my cloudberry syrup, which tastes almost like blackberries, with a perfect balance of sweetness and tartness.

3	orange slices
3	mint leaves
1½ oz.	gin
1 oz.	Cloudberry Syrup
¾ oz.	fresh lemon juice
	Ice cubes
1	orange wedge, to garnish

Muddle the orange slices and mint leaves ● Add the gin, syrup, and lemon juice ● Shake with ice to chill ● Strain into a rocks glass over fresh ice ● Garnish with the orange wedge ●

COACHELLA

A shimmery *Watermelon* SIPPER

Serves 1 No matter how bad a relationship gets, I hope we can all reach back in our memories and hold the beautiful days in our minds like shimmering gems—those times were real, too. For me, one of those times was when we went to our first Coachella together, in April of 2014. It was my second time ever going, and the lineup that year featured all our favorite bands, like Muse, Outkast, and Chromeo. It was incredible—being in the desert, surrounded by palm trees, beautiful sunsets, and the best music. But experiencing it with someone you are in love with brings another layer of magic. I felt so connected to him then. Even today, despite everything that happened, it is an amazing memory. In honor of those shiny, dazzling days, sip this cocktail that's bursting with watermelon and lime flavor, then showered with edible glitter.

NOTE ● I like adding a little CBD oil to this drink to amplify the relaxation vibes, but it tastes just as good without it, so I've listed it as an optional ingredient. Make sure to read the package directions on yours to ensure you're using the right dose.

2 oz.	vodka
3 oz.	watermelon juice
¾ oz.	fresh lime juice
½ oz.	grenadine (page 170)
1 dose	of your favorite CBD oil (optional, see Note)
1 dash	edible glitter, plus more for garnish
	Club soda, to top
	Ice cubes
	Small watermelon wedge, to garnish

Combine the vodka, watermelon juice, lime juice, grenadine, CBD oil, and glitter in a shaker tin ● Add ice and shake to chill ● Strain into a Collins glass, and top with club soda ● Garnish with the watermelon wedge and sprinkle with more glitter on top ●

(LOVE) BIRDS
in Paradise

TROPICAL *Mezcal Vibes*

Serves 4 Love can feel like an escape, and sometimes you need that even (or especially) after it's all burned up. One thing I've always enjoyed is experiencing new things; that's my definition of quality time with my person. When the show took us to film in Hawaii in 2015, we stayed a few days afterwards to have some fun in the sun, just the two of us. We rented a Jeep and drove up the long coast of Oahu's North Shore and saw all these beautiful places together. We went horseback riding, snorkeling, and diving with the sharks.

I remember thinking that this was the person I wanted to see the world with, whether it was just enjoying amazing food and drinks or doing crazy things like hanging out with sharks. This drink is an ode to those escapist times, those memories and moments in the sun.

The Jungle Bird is a tropical cocktail normally made with rum, but in this case I add fresh strawberries and a little mezcal because I love it so much; if that's not your thing, just swap in blackstrap rum for the mezcal!

4 oz.	aged rum
4 oz.	aged mezcal
2 oz.	Campari aperitivo
4 oz.	canned pineapple juice
4 oz.	fresh lime juice
4 oz.	simple syrup (page 170)
2	fresh strawberries
	Ice cubes
	Pineapple wedges, to garnish
12	maraschino cherries to garnish

Combine the rum, mezcal, Campari, juices, and syrup in a blender ● Add 2 cups of ice and the strawberries and blend until smooth, adding more ice gradually to reach your preferred consistency ● Strain into 4 of your best tiki mugs, then garnish each one with a pineapple wedge and 3 maraschino cherries on a cocktail pick ●

West
HOLLYWOOD

A truly TRASHY *Combo*

Serves 1 When we first lived together, it was in a real dumpster-fire of an apartment, which seems appropriate given where this all ended up. He had a place in West Hollywood, where he had lived for nearly 15 years before I moved in with him in April of 2015. It was his first apartment in Los Angeles and not the nicest—we couldn't do things like run the microwave and the air conditioner at the same time—but it was rent controlled and in the nicer part of the neighborhood. It made so much sense for us to live there while we saved money for a more permanent living arrangement. And though the place was a mess, we had a lot of happy memories there, too.

This combination of hard seltzer and Pedialyte kind of reminds me of old-school trash-can punch. Mix one up for yourself in a red Solo cup, or multiply the recipe and serve in a bucket, a pitcher, a punch bowl—even a trash can, why not? Enjoy it with friends when you're in a dumpster-fire state of mind.

1 packet of Pedialyte powder
1 can of your favorite hard seltzer
Ice cubes

Add the Pedialyte powder to a red Solo cup, then add the hard seltzer ● Stir to combine ● Add ice, and drink it up ●

High DOWN UNDER

LEMON, LIME,
Feel-Good
Times

2 oz.	vodka
½ oz.	fresh lemon juice
4 dashes	Angostura bitters
	Ice cubes
	Lemon-lime soda, to top
	Lemon twist, to garnish (optional)
	Lime twist, to garnish (optional)

Serves 1 This is a fizzy, bright sipper that will lift you up when you're feeling down. I love to travel, and there is nothing better than seeing the world with someone I love by my side. In 2016, we took my mom to Australia and New Zealand because it was her lifelong dream to visit these countries. He and I were so happy, totally in love with the places, and excited to take my mom there. The whole trip was so beautiful and such a thrill. I will always and forever cherish that memory.

In Australia, they have a drink called Lemon, Lime, and Bitters, made with lemon-lime soda and Angostura; it's very refreshing. In honor of that, this is a vodka-spiked version.

In a Collins glass, place the vodka, lemon juice, and bitters ● Add ice and stir briefly to combine ● Top with the lemon-lime soda and garnish with the lemon and lime twists, if desired ●

LOVE
& Marriage

RAISE YOUR
Own *Glass*

Serves 1 **When you're with someone for a long time, people inevitably start asking whether or not you're going to get married and have children. For me, I have never wanted either, but that answer never seems to be enough. There's always the follow-up question: Is it because I haven't met the right person yet? Nope, not that either! All that matters to me is being in a good relationship with someone I love and who loves me—no ring necessary.**

For all of you out there forging your own path to happiness, this fresh and flirty Champagne mimosa is for you.

2 oz.	lychee juice
4 oz.	fresh grapefruit juice
¼ oz.	simple syrup (page 170)
2 dashes	grapefruit bitters
	Champagne, to top
	Lemon twist, to garnish

Chill all ingredients for at least an hour ● Combine the lychee juice, grapefruit juice, simple syrup, and grapefruit bitters in a Champagne flute ● Stir briefly to combine ● Top with the Champagne, and garnish with a lemon twist ●

BREAK UP

Music means so much to me. From the good times to the terrible ones, there is no other artform that is as useful for connecting to your feelings. Musicians have been writing songs about heartbreak probably since the dawn of time, so there are hundreds of great songs out there to listen to when you're going through a bad breakup. Instead of sad ballads, I prefer to put on high-energy songs you can crank up to eleven. Why cry into your coffee when you can dance and scream it out instead? Here are ten of my favorite tracks. ●

MIX
TAPE

You Oughta Know
ALANIS MORRISETTE

Since You've Been Gone
KELLY CLARKSON

Toxic
BRITNEY SPEARS

Hold Up
BEYONCÉ

You've Done Enough
GORGON CITY + DRAMA

Traitor
OLIVIA RODRIGO

I'm Still Standing
ELTON JOHN

Heard It Through the Grapevine
MARVIN GAYE

Go Your Own Way
FLEETWOOD MAC

How to be a Heartbreaker
MARINA AND THE DIAMONDS

My Sweet HONEY

A HONEY-LACED
Tequila Highball

Serves 1 **For all the toxic, hurtful pain to come, there was sweetness, too—and this drink is a reminder of that. It was often hard to have our private lives unfold on the show; being in the spotlight can take a toll on even the strongest of couples. But while we had our fair share of tumultuous moments, I always found comfort in how we would turn toward each other during those times. When people attacked our relationship, he always made me feel safe and seen.**

This tequila highball balances zingy ginger beer with a ribbon of honey syrup—for my sweet honey that was.

1½ oz.	tequila
¾ oz.	fresh lemon juice
½ oz.	honey syrup (page 170)
	Ice cubes
	Ginger beer, to top

Combine the tequila, lemon juice, and honey syrup in a shaker tin with ice and shake to chill ● Strain into a Collins glass, and top with the ginger beer ●

TOGETHER
Forever

CHEERS
to a
Bright Future

Serves 1 **This is the perfect cocktail for toasting special occasions, the big happy milestones. Owning property has always been a dream of mine, and I knew I wanted to do it with my life partner. In 2018, we had finally saved up enough money to buy a house. We looked at maybe thirty different places, but when we walked into the house in Valley Village, I knew right away that it was the one. I was struggling to have a poker face in front of the agent, because it was so perfect. It was our dream home. When we got the keys, it was the most joyous experience, our together-forever moment. I could see the next fifty years of my life unfold with this person. Regardless of whether the house would remain with us or not, I knew that we would remain together.**

For celebratory times like those, whip up this toast-worthy drink that includes bergamot-laced Italicus liqueur for a little extra oomph and sparkle.

NOTE ● If you don't have Italicus, or don't want to use it, this also tastes great with St-Germain elderflower liqueur.

¾ OZ.	Italicus Rosolio di Bergamotto aperitivo
	Champagne, to top

Chill all ingredients for at least an hour ● Add the Italicus to a Champagne flute ● Top with Champagne ● Taste the drink—if it is too dry, you can add more Italicus in ¼ ounce increments ●

Sunday RITUAL

An ORANGE WINE *Sangria*

Serves 1 This is sunshine in a glass—a joyful, fruit-forward drink for laidback Sundays. As a kid, my family would always have a big family dinner on Sundays. My mom would pull out all the stops, or my dad would grill, and no matter what was happening in the world, we would look forward to it every week.

Once he and I got settled in our house in Valley Village, I wanted to start that as our tradition, too. While we cooked, I'd put on what I called my "Sunday music"—one of my favorite bands, War on Drugs. We would drink wine and listen to music, with phones down, no distractions. The windows would be open, breeze coming in, dogs walking around. The two of us just connecting. Those memories in our dream kitchen together were the best quality times. It was so pure, and I always wanted more of that for us.

This recipe is formatted for one, in case you're living your best slow weekend days solo. To enjoy with friends, simply multiply the measurements by the number of people you're serving.

NOTE ● Traditional sangria is made with red wine, but I like the tanginess of orange wine, which goes especially well with tropical fruits like pineapple; mix and match your favorite fruits to find what works for you. This drink would also taste great with Cocchi Americano in place of the Lillet.

4	fresh pineapple chunks, about 1-inch by 1-inch, peeled
½	orange, halved
½	lemon, halved
6 oz.	orange wine (see Note)
1 oz.	Lillet Rosé apéritif
¾ oz.	simple syrup (page 170)
	Ice cubes
	Fresh fruits, like pineapple, oranges, golden berries

In a shaker tin, muddle the pineapple, orange, and lemon ● Add the wine, Lillet, and syrup ● Gently shake with ice to combine ● You don't have to go big here—just shake enough to get everything mixed up together nicely ● Strain into a wineglass over fresh ice and garnish with an array of fresh fruits ●

INTIMACY Issues

RYE WHISKEY meets *lemon & mint*

2	mint sprigs
½	lemon, cut into quarters
2 oz.	rye whiskey
¾ oz.	simple syrup (page 170)
¼ oz.	Cointreau liqueur
	Ice cubes
	Crushed ice
	Lemon peel, to garnish

Serves 1 Every relationship needs work, whether you realize it at the time or not. When I first came into ours, things were shiny, beautiful, and great. Then, as the honeymoon phase started to wear off, my issues from my past relationship started to creep back in; I had been previously dating someone who was emotionally and verbally abusive. I had a lot of anxiety, and it took tons of hard work to rewrite the story of my self-worth in my head. He supported me through it, while there was a totally false narrative in the media that we had no physical intimacy in our relationship. He didn't know exactly how to help me, but he had a desire to help, and that meant a lot.

This simple whiskey smash needs that extra effort, too; put a little elbow grease into your muddle to really get all the lemon oils into the drink.

Muddle the lemon wedges and mint sprigs together in a shaker tin ● Add the rye whiskey, simple syrup, Cointreau, and ice cubes ● Shake it like you mean it, to thoroughly chill the drink ● Set the prepared cocktail aside and fill a rocks glass with crushed ice ● Strain the cocktail over crushed ice ● Garnish with the lemon peel ●

Solo SESSIONS

A REFRESHING
Alcohol-Free *Cooler*

Serves 1 Sans alcohol, this drink will reinvigorate you when you need it most. I have always been a huge proponent of going to therapy. During the pandemic, in 2020 and 2021, I went every week. I had one therapist who was really good at helping me get out of my own way to reach my personal goals. We talked about my relationship during those solo sessions, but the focus was really on my anxiety and depression, and how those things were holding me back from achieving what I wanted to accomplish. I found it incredibly helpful. I highly recommend therapy for anyone who has these struggles too.

This is an alcohol-free cocktail made with fresh cucumber and herbs. Just like a good therapy session, you walk away feeling lighter and optimistic about the future after drinking it.

3	cucumber slices
2	fresh basil leaves, plus an extra leaf to garnish
2	mint sprigs
2 oz.	Ritual zero-proof tequila
¾ oz.	fresh lime juice
¾ oz.	simple syrup (page 170)
	Ice cubes
	Club soda, to top

Muddle the cucumber, basil, and mint in the bottom of a shaker tin ● Add the zero-proof tequila, lime juice, and syrup ● Shake with ice to chill ● Strain into a Collins glass and top with the club soda ● Garnish with a basil leaf ●

Little Sister VIBES

Shirley Temple with A SHIV

Serves 1 When I was a kid, I loved a good Shirley Temple, cherry red and cloyingly sweet. This boozy version of that childhood drink, made with the addition of vodka, may seem girlish and innocent, but it's anything but. When I first met the woman he had the affair with, she was dating someone who was close with my brother. As our groups started to mingle more, I got to know her better. At first, she came across as timid and afraid to speak her mind, and I think there were people who wanted to ice her out, or keep her away. I hated to see that, so Scheana and I took her under our wing. We introduced her to people, went dancing together—and even wore matching outfits on Halloween. We really embraced her as one of our own, like a little sister.

Serve these up when you need a throwback to simpler, more naïve times, but watch out—it may sneak up on you.

3	fresh cherries
¾ oz.	grenadine (page 170)
2 oz.	vodka
¾ oz.	fresh lime juice
	Ice cubes
	Club soda, to top
1	maraschino cherry, to garnish

In a shaker tin, muddle the fresh cherries with the grenadine ● Add the vodka and lime juice ● Add ice and shake to chill ● Strain into a Collins glass over fresh ice ● Top with the club soda and garnish with the maraschino cherry—use the neon red kind for nostalgia's sake ●

BETRA

YAL

the slow drip of deception

Midlife

Smoke

COUPLES The

Home *for*

WATCH What

Explosion 1

Revenge PORN 1

Ra

Midlife
CRISIS

A SMOLDERING SHOT
of *Cinnamon Spice*

Serves 1 **This fiery shot made with cinnamon-spiked Fireball whisky and overproof rum burns all the way down.**

Before he turned 40, he started going through a midlife crisis that was accelerated by the pandemic, when everybody was in lockdown. It was the match that would go on to incinerate our partnership, home, friendships—all just so he could feel younger. I remember that out of the blue, he wanted to stay out all the time, and he rebelled against doing anything that required a certain level of responsibility. He shopped for flashy new cars and started wearing clothes he thought made him look younger. I'm not sure he recognized what was happening, but it was obvious to me. It was all very unfortunate at the time but realizing that the affair was a part of it put it all into a darker perspective.

Down this shot to feel the flames.

1 oz. Fireball Cinnamon Whisky
Wray & Nephew white
   overproof rum, to top

Pour the whiskey into a shot glass ● Top with a very thin layer of rum ●

Smoke & MIRRORS

A SWEET DRINK with a *sour bite*

Serves 1 If you've been cheated on in a relationship, one of the most difficult things is to eventually learn about the multiple points of deception that took place—the countless times smoke and mirrors were put in front of you.

One night we hosted a party at our house with a bunch of friends. It was late, everyone was drinking, so she stayed in the guest bedroom to avoid having to drive home. In the middle of the night, I woke up and couldn't find him anywhere, so I went downstairs and checked almost every single room. As I was walking down the hallway I saw him leave the guest bedroom. He said he heard her walking around and just wanted to check if she needed water or anything.

A part of me instinctively knew that wasn't the truth. I told him I believed him anyway and we all know what came next.

NOTE ● The egg whites in this mezcal blackberry sour create a nice fluffy texture, but if eggs aren't your thing, whip up some aquafaba (page 171) instead—the vegan-friendly ingredient adds the same lightness.

7	blackberries
¾ oz.	vanilla syrup (page 171)
1	egg white or 1 oz. aquafaba (see Note)
¾ oz.	fresh lime juice
2 dashes	Angostura bitters
2 oz.	mezcal
	Ice cubes

In the bottom of a shaker tin, muddle 4 of the blackberries with the vanilla syrup ● Add the egg white, lime juice, bitters, and mezcal ● Shake (without ice) to combine the ingredients ● Add ice and shake again to chill ● Strain into a coupe glass ● Garnish with three blackberries on a cocktail pick ●

COUPLES Therapy

A DECEPTIVE and delicious

Espresso Martini

Serves 1 The espresso martini has made a comeback in recent years, but this one is made with decaf espresso. It has all the brash appearance of the original but without the promise of a caffeine buzz—a cocktail bait-and-switch.

He ran his own con game on me, of course, and one of the biggest betrayals was when we started going to couples therapy together in late 2022. He was in the thick of his midlife crisis while trying to open a bar, and as we had more serious talks about the state of our relationship, he suggested couples therapy. I thought it was a great idea and we should totally do it. In the first session, he had a laundry list of things to unload on me. It was a lot to take in, but I considered it a good step forward in our relationship. I trusted him completely.

Since then, he's revealed that he only suggested seeing the therapist after he began the affair, because he wanted to break up with me there. I still believe in couples therapy, but it works only if you both bring honesty to the table.

1 oz.	decaf espresso, fully cooled
2 oz.	vodka
½ oz.	coffee liqueur
½ oz.	vanilla syrup (page 171)
1 dash	chocolate bitters (optional)
	Ice cubes
	Coffee beans, to garnish

Add the espresso to a shaker tin, then add the vodka, coffee liqueur, syrup, and bitters (if using) ● Shake with ice to chill ● Strain into a martini glass and garnish with the coffee beans ●

WARNING signs

Spotting an affair isn't always easy, but in my experience there are a few red flags to look for in regards to your significant other.

- Starting a cover band
- A new or increased obsession with fitness
- Turning off shared location
- Suddenly acting protective of their phone
- Friends badgering you about your sex life

BONNIE

A FLORAL *Love Letter*

with gin and crème de violette

Serves 1 My grandmother Bonnie was born in 1929 and she passed away in September 2022. She was an absolute force to be reckoned with—fiercely independent, one of my best friends, and someone I really looked up to. I always wanted to spend more time with her, and even when she was ninety-three years old, we would still FaceTime together often. The day she passed, a green Amazon parrot flew into our back window. We took the parrot in for a few days and eventually found its owners, but I kept thinking that nothing more meaningful could have happened at that moment. I have always believed that birds carry something from the spirit world, and my mom has suggested that my grandma sent that bird to us.

I didn't know the affair was happening at this time, but I find a lot of comfort in remembering that little gift my grandma sent us that day. This floral drink is an homage to her beautiful spirit.

2 oz.	Hendrick's gin
¾ oz.	fresh lemon juice
¾ oz.	simple syrup (page 170)
¼ oz.	crème de violette
	Ice cubes
	Lemon peel, to garnish

Combine the gin, lemon juice, syrup, and liqueur in a shaker tin, then add ice and shake to chill ● Strain into a coupe glass and garnish with the lemon peel ●

HOME for the Holidays

A FESTIVE

Moscow Mule

Serves 1 Holidays can be a particularly tough time post-breakup. Remembering those special days together is hard, but for me, knowing what happened when we were apart then has been even worse.

His family lives in St. Louis, and I'm from Florida, so the holidays were always a challenge, trying to figure out how to see everybody together. Since my grandmother passed away in September 2022, my mom came out to Los Angeles to be with us for Christmas. We had a special time going out to dinner and fun bars, riding on the gondolas, and seeing the Christmas lights together. It meant so much to me after my grandmother's death. He then left on Christmas Eve to see his family while I stayed in L.A. with my mom. I found out later that he flew his affair partner out to his hometown to spend that time between Christmas and New Year's together.

This drink—a Moscow mule with a little pomegranate syrup and cranberry gin liqueur—will lift your holiday spirit and bring that special sparkle to your festivities when you need it most.

1 oz.	Koval cranberry gin liqueur
1½ oz.	vodka
½ oz.	grenadine (page 170)
½ oz.	fresh lemon juice
	Ice cubes
	Ginger beer, to top
	Mint sprig, to garnish

In a shaker tin, combine the cranberry liqueur with the vodka, grenadine, and lemon juice ● Shake with ice to chill ● Strain into a Moscow mule mug and top with the ginger beer ● Garnish with a mint sprig ●

Watch What HAPPENS

A HOT MESS *Hot Toddy*

Serves 1 When you've been betrayed, it's painful to think back on memories and know that something completely different was going on.

Watch What Happens Live is the show Andy Cohen does every night after the primetime Bravo shows. Usually one or two cast members from our show fly to New York for the taping to dish on all the events that unfolded in the episode. For the premiere of Season 10, my ex and his best friend did the show, and when I watched it later, I noticed his friend was acting strange. I found out later that my ex's affair partner was in New York during that time—he had flown her out for the day, and she was in his hotel room while the show filmed. To recall how I helped him pick out outfits for the trip and kissed him goodbye before he went to the airport is devastating—and now I know why his best friend was acting so weird.

A simple hot toddy will comfort and warm you inside and out, and the use of Jäger instead of whiskey in this drink turns up the hot-mess factor.

NOTE ● If you don't like the licorice flavor of Jäger, you can sub in any other amaro, or whiskey, rum, or brandy.

2 oz.	Jägermeister herbal liqueur (see Note)
¾ oz.	honey syrup (page 170)
¾ oz.	fresh lemon juice
6 to 7 oz.	hot water, to taste
	Lemon peel, to garnish

Combine the Jägermeister, honey syrup, lemon juice, and hot water in a hot mug and stir to blend the ingredients ● When working with hot water, be sure not to burn yourself! ● Garnish with the lemon peel ●

EXPLOSION

STORMY like a *Hurricane*

1 oz.	dark rum
1 oz.	light rum
¾ oz.	fresh lime juice
¾ oz.	passion fruit juice
¾ oz.	black tea syrup (page 170)
	Ice cubes
	Orange wedge, to garnish
	Strawberry, to garnish

Serves 1 The moment a relationship truly breaks can feel like a hurricane has hit. For me, it was the night I found out about the affair. We all went to TomTom to support his cover band, and while he was performing, his phone fell out of his pocket. Our mutual friend got up and grabbed it, and gave it to me to hold. After the show, I felt a bolt of lightning shoot down my spine—a flash of intuition that I needed to look at his phone. I went to the bathroom and started looking at stuff, and that's when I found the screen recording of him and his affair partner having sex.

I was shaking with feelings of shock, anger, disbelief, and hurt. I thought I was going to puke. I busted out of the stall and confronted him. There was a lot of yelling, and I ended up calling her and begging her to tell me when this had started. This drink, my take on a hurricane, is an ode to that moment.

Combine the rums, fruit juices, and syrup in a shaker tin with ice and shake to chill ● Strain into a hurricane glass ● Garnish with an orange wedge and strawberry ●

WRECKING BALL

A RESTORATIVE
Bloody Mary

	Lemon wedge
	Celery salt, to rim the glass
2 oz.	vodka
1 oz.	fresh lemon juice
¼ oz.	Worcestershire sauce
½ oz.	pickle juice
	Ice cubes
	Tomato juice, to top

To Finish

Kosher salt

Black pepper

Tabasco sauce

Pickles (such as cornichons, dill spears, pickled carrots, pickled baby corn, or pickled jalapeños), to garnish

Serves 1 For the few days following my discovery of the affair, things between us were extremely contentious. He yelled at me all the time, getting mad whenever I questioned him. He was indignant and dismissive of the whole thing, as if somehow this was unfair to him. I couldn't wrap my head around the way he was acting, because it was almost like I wasn't allowed to be upset. All of that really messed with my head. He was the worst version of himself during this time, a wrecking ball to my life.

This bloody mary is great for picking yourself up after the wreckage of a long night of drinking. It will leave you standing tall on the other side.

Prepare your glass by running a lemon wedge along the rim ● Dip the rim in the celery salt ● Inside the glass, combine the vodka, lemon juice, Worcestershire, and pickle juice ● Add ice and stir briefly to chill ● Top with the tomato juice ● To finish, season with salt, pepper, and Tabasco sauce, to your taste ● Garnish to your heart's desire ●

REVENGE Porn

 A VIRGIN *Martini*

Serves 1 Being betrayed may leave you with an intense desire for vengeance, but I always tried to rise above it all, even when I felt so deeply hurt and angry. After I confronted him about the affair, her lawyers sent me cease-and-desist letters, thinking I would distribute their sex tape. I would never do that, despite all the pain I felt, because at the end of the day, I can't imagine doing something so horrible.

This is a take on the porn star martini, the modern classic made with vanilla vodka, passion fruit, and sometimes a sidecar of sparkling wine. My version is zero-proof, so it is made with a non-alcoholic spirit and wine—it has the same bite as the real deal, but without the collateral damage.

2 oz.	Seedlip Grove 42
¾ oz.	passion fruit juice
¾ oz.	fresh lime juice
¾ oz.	vanilla syrup (page 171)
	Ice cubes
	Passion fruit slice, to garnish (optional)
2 oz.	non-alcoholic sparkling wine or club soda

Add the Seedlip, passion fruit juice, lime juice, vanilla syrup, and ice to a shaker tin and shake until chilled ● Strain into a coupe glass ● Garnish with the passion fruit slice ● Pour the non-alcoholic sparkling wine into a sidecar or shot glass and serve on the side ●

The FUNERAL

A HEAVYWEIGHT *Amaro Punch*

4 oz.	Averna amaro
4 oz.	gin
3 oz.	fresh lime juice
2 oz.	simple syrup (page 170)
	Ice cubes
4	lime wheels, to garnish
4	maraschino cherries, to garnish

Serves 4 After the news of the affair broke, all my friends showed up for me. They brought flowers and wine. There were probably twenty people at my house at one point, all offering me support. He was at her apartment at the time, and when he finally came back to the house, he started yelling at everybody to leave, angry that our friends were there for me, not him. He referred to it as a party at the time, but it wasn't a party—it was a funeral for our relationship.

This frozen punch made with gin and amaro is perfect for when your friends show up—and they will—to mourn and rally.

Combine the amaro, gin, lime juice, and syrup in a blender with 2 cups of ice ● Blend on low, gradually increasing the speed as the ingredients start to turn into slush ● When completely smooth, pour into punch cups ● Garnish with the lime wheels and cherries ●

RAT Poison

A DEADLY *Combination*

½ oz.	Jim Beam bourbon whiskey
½ oz.	Jack Daniel's Tennessee whiskey
½ oz.	Johnny Walker Scotch whiskey
½ oz.	Jose Cuervo tequila
½ oz.	Jägermeister herbal liqueur
½ oz.	Rose's lime juice

Serves 3 **When the rats start infesting your life, you've got to get them the hell out of there fast, and sometimes the best way to do that is to make them the most disgusting cocktail they've ever had. Based on the classic Four Horsemen shot, which includes four types of whiskey, this drink isn't about using great ingredients, because it's not going to taste good any way you look at it. It's about grabbing whatever you can find on the bottom shelf and shooting it back quickly. Hand it to the Rat King in your life or down it to rid yourself of spiritual vermin. Ex-termination complete.**

No need to get fancy with this one ● Just pour the whiskeys, tequila, Jägermeister, and lime juice into a shaker tin with ice and shake to chill ● Strain into shot glasses to serve ●

ATION

breaking down, to build again

The Real
TRUTH

A DECEPTIVELY SPICY *Cherry Manhattan*

Serves 1 This cherry Manhattan looks nice and sweet at first glance, but thanks to the spicy bitters, it burns a little after the first few sips, just like how it feels to find out the truths of a broken relationship. About a month after everything came out, the real stories began to drip out, little by little. Her following him around the country when he was touring with his cover band. Him asking people to pay for things on their credit cards so the charges wouldn't show up on his bank statements. Each story was a cigarette burn on the life I once knew.

2 oz.	bourbon
1 oz.	sweet vermouth
½ oz.	cherry liqueur
2 dashes	chili bitters
	Ice cubes
	Maraschino cherry, to garnish

Combine the bourbon, vermouth, liqueur, and bitters in a mixing glass with ice ● Stir to chill ● Strain into a coupe glass ● Garnish with the cherry ●

Who KNEW

A STINGER with a
touch of sweetness

Serves 1 **This drink is inspired by the classic stinger cocktail. I've added fruity liqueur to make it sting just a little less, because we should show ourselves a bit of kindness in times like I had. It turned out a lot of people knew about the affair before I did. Nobody deserves the pressure of keeping a secret that isn't theirs, and it makes me upset that he put them in that position. Some of them have apologized to me since, and it breaks my heart to hear how heavy it was on them. I am not angry at those friends, but I do wish someone would have come forward earlier with the truth. If you've gone through this too, try this softened-up stinger as a temporary salve.**

    NOTE ● The quality of this cocktail hinges entirely on the caliber of ingredients you choose, so don't be cheap!

2 oz.	brandy
½ oz.	white crème de menthe
½ oz.	cherry liqueur
	Ice cubes

Combine the brandy, crème de menthe, and cherry liqueur in a mixing glass with ice and stir to chill ● Make sure you stir the drink longer than feels natural because it's best served ultra-cold ● Strain into a martini glass ●

RUMORS

A BITTERSWEET
Absinthe Swizzle

1½ oz.	absinthe
1½ oz.	canned pineapple juice
¾ oz.	fresh lime juice
¾ oz.	falernum liqueur
	Crushed ice
½ oz.	crème de cassis
	Mint bouquet, to garnish

Serves 1 Over the course of our relationship, there were rumors that constantly hovered over us like a dark cloud. Rumors that we had an open relationship or that we were faking it for the camera, or that I was gay, or that we suffered from a complete lack of physical intimacy; none of these things are true. However, now I know there were other rumors that *were* true—like the affair. In this cocktail mixed with a swizzle stick for an extra dose of chaos, the dark red float of crème de cassis on top seeps down into the drink, the same way insidious rumors spread through a crowd, whether they are true or not.

In a Collins glass, add the absinthe, pineapple, lime juice, and liqueur ● Fill the glass with crushed ice and swizzle to chill ● Top with more crushed ice ● Float the crème de cassis on top of the drink, slowly, so it trickles down into the drink gradually ● Garnish with a mint bouquet ●

"Separate LIVES"

COFFEE and CREAM,
alone together

Serves 1 The flavors in this drink—the coffee liqueur and heavy cream—complement and contrast each other, existing both separately and together. Throughout our relationship, I truly believed that we were in it together, our lives deeply intertwined. This drink name is in quotes because he now refers to us as having separate lives. From my perspective, I had no reason to think that—we had always been in good communication, slept in the same bed together, and even when we were apart, I helped him do things like pick out an outfit for a trip. For him to make it seem like our breakup wasn't that bad because we lived separate lives is a painful form of justification for his actions. This drink represents how alone I actually was in our relationship despite being together.

¾ oz.	tequila
¾ oz.	vodka
¾ oz.	coffee liqueur
¾ oz.	Averna amaro
	Ice cubes
1 oz.	heavy cream
	Chocolate bitters, to garnish
	Cocoa powder, to garnish

In a shaker tin, combine the tequila, vodka, coffee liqueur, and amaro ● Add ice and shake to chill ● Strain into a coupe or Irish coffee glass ● Top with heavy cream, then add a few drops of the chocolate bitters on top ● Garnish with a dusting of cocoa powder ●

THE BEST DRINKS TO THROW IN SOMEONE'S

● **Champagne** is a great option because when it dries it smells awful. ● **Sauvignon Blanc** won't leave a mark—no evidence, no crime? ● **Cabernet Sauvignon** *will* leave a stain, so use wisely. ● **Cheap Beer,** preferably lukewarm, will leave them as damp and smelly as a frat basement. ● **Frozen Piña Colada** for a shocking polar bear plunge to the face, and all that sugar will leave a sticky mess. ● **Sambuca** smells so gross—whenever someone ordered it at the bar I'd have to plug my nose. ● **Bloody Mary** because why wait until evening to throw a drink in a bar when you can start at brunch? ● **Pisco Sour** for literal egg on their face.

Just make sure you only throw the liquid and not the glass or bottle—the idea isn't to actually inflict pain, just to embarrass the hell out of them.

DOUBLE Life

A DUO of NAUGHTY & NICE *Shots*

Naughty		
½ oz.	Jeppson's Malört liqueur (see Note)
½ oz.	fresh grapefruit juice
½ oz.	honey
	Ice cubes

Nice		
½ oz.	Irish whiskey
½ oz.	crème de cacao
½ oz.	coffee liqueur
	Ice cubes

Serves 1 I tried to be a loving, trusting girlfriend, and though we weren't in a state of bliss the entire time, I was always committed to working on the relationship when things got hard. Did he ever afford me that luxury? In reality, he was constantly showing me one person and sneaking off to be another person with her, whether it was during my grandmother's funeral, at a music festival with all our friends, or a wedding in Mexico.

This duo of shots represents those two people I now know existed within him and the double life he was living—the sweet chocolatey one when he was pretending we were cool, and the other a deeply bitter shot of deception. Choose one or the other depending on your mood, or down them both back-to-back for a head-spinning, two-faced effect.

NOTE ● If you can't stand the bitter taste of Malört, Jägermeister also works in the naughty shot.

For each shot, combine the ingredients in a shaker tin with ice and shake to chill ● Strain each into a shot glass ●

JAMIE

A DIRTY
as
HELL
Martini

Serves 1 In contrast to the elegant Vesper-inspired martini that began our story (page 22), this one is as dirty as it gets, perfect for when you're feeling the briny muck of your breakup.

Throughout the affair, he did a lot of shit to me that was dirty as hell, but some things really felt like new lows. He had told me time and time again that he wasn't trying to hide anything from me whenever I would ask about little things here and there. But it turns out he was taking many steps to cover the whole thing up. He was so committed to this double life that he used "Jamie" as a code name for her in his phone.

The worst part is that my dad's name was James, may he rest in peace. Imagine seeing a screenshot of a text in which he tells a friend how he "took Jamie to the mile high club." For him to use my dad's name for her was a level of disrespect I didn't realize was possible.

2½ oz.	vodka
½ to ¾ oz.	olive juice, to your liking
	Ice cubes
	Olives or pickled onions, to garnish

Combine the vodka and olive juice in a mixing glass with ice and stir to chill ● Use a straw to taste the drink and make sure you are happy with the amount of olive juice included ● If you like it extra *extra* dirty, add a little more! ● Garnish with a skewer of olives (my personal favorite), pickled cocktail onions, or hell, you could do both ●

Crocodile TEARS

PRETTY IN PINK, but *Wickedly Bitter*

1 oz.	Campari aperitivo
1 oz.	gin
¾ oz.	fresh lemon juice
¾ oz.	simple syrup (page 170)
1 bar spoon	maraschino liqueur
	Ice cubes
2 dashes	orange bitters, to garnish

Serves 1 This pretty pink cocktail looks nice and sweet, but since it's made with Campari and grapefruit bitters, that innocence is just a façade—crocodile tears in a coupe.

The number of falsehoods that came to light after the affair was diabolical. The affair was not a one-time event but a regular, ongoing thing. She met his family over the holidays without my knowing. They hooked up in our house while I was out of town for my grandmother's funeral—one of the absolute worst details. It goes on. Someday with distance maybe I'll have sympathy, but from where I sit, it doesn't get any more personal or hurtful.

Place the Campari, gin, lemon juice, syrup, and liqueur in a shaker, then add ice ● Shake hard to chill then strain into a coupe glass, making sure you don't let any ice chips sneak through the strainer into the drink ● Garnish with the dashes of orange bitters ●

GASLIGHT

A SHIFTY
Ginger Sidecar
that snaps

Serves 1 I always trusted my perception of things, but now I know he was doing everything he could to gaslight me into believing there was nothing going on behind the scenes. Not only that, he would turn it around on me, making me feel bad for even questioning him. I gave him plenty of opportunities to tell me the truth about the affair. I was being straight-up lied to in those moments, and he would always go out of his way to try to make me feel like I was crazy for asking any questions in the first place.

    This drink seems like a sidecar—the classic cocktail with brandy, Cointreau, and lemon juice—and while you may expect the traditional version, in reality there's something different about it while you sip. The ginger brings in a rough, spicy element that bites, and the black tea syrup adds a dark underlying complexity.

2 slices	fresh ginger
2 oz.	Cognac
¼ oz.	Cointreau liqueur
¾ oz.	fresh lemon juice
¾ oz.	black tea syrup (page 170)
	Ice cubes
	Lemon peel, to garnish

Muddle the ginger slices in a shaker tin, then add the Cognac, Cointreau, lemon juice, and tea syrup ● Add ice and shake to chill ● Strain into a martini glass ● Garnish with the lemon peel ●

Lack of REMORSE

THE DEVIL, in *liquid form*

2 oz.	Ritual zero-proof tequila
¾ oz.	grenadine (page 170)
¾ oz.	fresh lime juice
	Ice cubes
	High-quality tonic water, to top (see Note)
	Lime wheel, to garnish

Serves 1 When someone you loved and spent your life with hurts you to this extent, it's like that person you once knew transformed into an unreal, nightmarish thing. What's worse is when there is a serious lack of remorse for those actions. Ever since he got caught having the affair, sometimes there are moments when it seems like he might feel bad about what he did—but they are fleeting. Instead, he chooses to say all sorts of terrible things about our relationship, doubling down on showing the world who he really was all along—the devil in my life. Drink this alcohol-free remix of the classic El Diablo cocktail and exorcise that shit.

NOTE ● It's important to use high-quality tonic water in this recipe (not your average grocery store brands, which tend to have more sugar). If not, your drink may taste too sweet. I love Q tonic water for this reason.

Combine the zero-proof tequila, grenadine, and lime juice in a shaker tin with ice ● Shake to chill ● Strain into a Collins glass ● Add ice, then top with the tonic water ● Garnish with the lime wheel ●

SNAKE in the GRASS

A DAIQUIRI that  *Bites Back*

Serves 1 This is a twist on a simple daiquiri for when you're hurt by the ones you least expect. It's one thing to be betrayed your partner, but the fact that it involved my friend took it to a whole other level of deception. I have to admit, I definitely infantilized her and did not see her as capable of any of this wreckage. Not only because of how she acted, and who she was and what she looked like, but because she was so integrated into our friends group. She always wanted to spend time together and I was there for her when she had her own problems with guys, including ones she was seeing while she was with my boyfriend. Though she operated as my friend, she was stabbing me in the back the whole time.

NOTE ● This drink was inspired by the classic daiquiri. It features the Brazilian cane spirit cachaça because I like the way it brings a grassy element to the flavor, but you can substitute any rum you like. Try spiced rum, or unaged rum for a more straightforward version.

2 oz.	cachaça liquor (see Note)
¾ oz.	fresh lime juice
¾ oz.	simple syrup (page 170)
	Ice cubes
	Lime wedge, to garnish

Place the cachaça, lime juice, and syrup in a shaker tin and add ice ● Shake to chill ● Strain into a coupe glass and garnish with the lime wedge ●

INFOR-MATION Booth

A SOPHISTICATED show of
Intelligence

Serves 1 During our relationship, he used to refer to me as an "information booth" because I liked keeping up with the news and what was going on with the world and our friends. He was the opposite and just not the most aware person, so he would come to me for news and info. I always thought the nickname was a compliment, but in the aftermath of our breakup he has brought it up in interviews as an example of how I intentionally made him feel dumb. In retrospect, it feels like he was waiting to use it against me.

No woman should dumb herself down for anyone. Own your intelligence and power. Toast to yourself with this drink, a heavy pour of a badass spirit of your choice—for me that's going to be a really nice bottle of Japanese whisky.

2 oz. of your favorite, most luxurious spirit
Ice cube
Citrus peel, to garnish (optional)

Pour your favorite spirit into the most beautiful glass you own ● Add a large ice cube ● If you're feeling extra fancy, you could add a citrus peel garnish for a pop of color (I like orange peel paired with whisky) ●

STRANGER in My Life

A soothing

HOT TEA
Cocktail

1	black tea bag
6 oz.	boiling water
2 oz.	dark rum (see Note)
¾ oz.	fresh lemon juice
¾ oz.	honey syrup (page 170)
	Orange peel studded with cloves, to garnish

Serves 1 When everything you knew about your partner and your relationship is flipped on its head, that shakes you to your core. After the news of the affair broke, we continued to live in the same house together, but now it felt like I was living with a stranger. I always thought he had good intentions and cared deeply about me, but now I can't say that I even know who he is anymore. Continuing to live so closely together, hearing him walking in the hallway or talking in the kitchen, caused me a lot of anxiety.

Who is this person I slept next to for the last nine years? What was I not seeing? I spent almost a decade with him and now he is a complete stranger. Whenever I feel this uneasiness, I turn to a cup of hot tea, a glass of comfort just like this one.

NOTE ● If you aren't in the mood for rum, you can use an alcohol-free spirit of your choice, or totally omit the booze.

Brew the black tea first by combining the tea bag and boiling water in a mug and letting it steep for at least one minute ● Remove the tea bag ● Pour the rum into the mug, followed by the lemon juice ● Stir in the honey syrup until it dissolves ● Garnish with the orange peel studded with a few cloves ●

Tears ON YOUR GRAVE

A SALTY *Good* Riddance

	Grapefruit wedge, to rim the glass
	Kosher salt, to rim the glass
2 oz.	vodka
¾ oz.	Aperol aperitivo
1 oz.	fresh grapefruit juice
¾ oz.	fresh lime juice
¾ oz.	rosemary syrup (page 171)
1 to 2 dashes	grapefruit bitters
	Ice cubes
	Grapefruit wheel, to garnish

Serves 1 There is sadness with any breakup, but when it ends in a way that blows up friendships and relationships in the most toxic way possible, it's a little different. I have no interest in speaking to either one of them again, or to mourn the passing of our relationship with love or respect. I'm not leaving flowers on this grave; instead, I'm leaving tears and walking away with my strength.

This drink is reminiscent of a Salty Dog cocktail, with a little Aperol for a hint of the sunshine to come.

Prepare the Collins glass by running a grapefruit wedge along the rim ● Dip the wet rim in salt and set aside ● In a shaker tin, add the vodka, Aperol, citrus juices, syrup, and bitters ● Add ice and shake to chill ● Strain into the prepared Collins glass over fresh ice ● Garnish with the grapefruit wheel ●

ENCE

SUPPORT
System

TO SHARE with the
Best of the Best

Serves 4 After I found out about the affair, things were really bad. I wasn't eating or sleeping. Meredith, my best friend from college, was the first person to show up. She called out from work, showed up at my home, and rallied an incredible bunch of friends to help me through this time. She started a text group called the Madix Support Team, and set up a spreadsheet that coordinated who would stay with me every night; she is a Capricorn queen and one of the most organized people I know.

There was someone always here—whether it was Meredith, Logan, Brad, or Dana—who was ready and willing to spend the night so I wasn't here just by myself with my ex in the guest room. They supported me like this for weeks. That was such a beautiful thing: to know these people were going to be there for me through thick and thin. This drink is a toast to them—a frozen tropical punch for besties only.

NOTE ● If sunflower orgeat isn't your thing, you can buy a commercial orgeat at the liquor store or online that will also taste great in this cocktail.

8 oz.	gin
2 oz.	fresh lemon juice
2 oz.	passion fruit juice
2 oz.	sunflower orgeat syrup (page 171, or see Note)
2 oz.	falernum liqueur
	Ice cubes
	Pineapple wedge and leaf, to garnish

To make the drink, combine the gin, lemon juice, passion fruit juice, syrup, and falernum in a blender with 2 cups of ice ● Blend on low, gradually increasing the speed as the ingredients start to turn into slush ● When completely smooth, pour into tiki mugs and garnish each glass with a pineapple wedge and leaf ●

ROSE Quartz

A SPARKLING PINK *Spritz*

Serves 1 I have always been open about my anxiety, and in the aftermath of this affair it had never been worse. I had this huge pit in my stomach for weeks. I didn't sleep. I couldn't stop the anxious feelings. Thankfully, I had friends who brought me healing candles and crystals, including a rose quartz for emotional support from my friend Simon. I would press it against my solar plexus and hold it there for hours. I continued to use it during the toughest times to come, including my trip to Mexico and coming home for the reunion, just trying to will the knot in my stomach to go away. As it started to get better, I thought, okay, the worst thing that could have happened did happen, which makes the rest start to feel doable. Anything else that comes, I can handle it because the worst is behind me.

I'm not going to say I'm cured, but when we go through an ordeal like this, it shows us that we can handle so much more than we thought we could. Realizing that has helped me feel less anxious than ever before. In honor of that pretty rose quartz, this is a sparkling rosé spritz—a refreshing source of hope during dark times.

1 oz.	Aperol aperitivo
1 oz.	Lillet Rosé apéritif
1 to 2 dashes	grapefruit bitters (optional)
	Ice cubes
4 oz.	sparkling rosé
2 oz.	club soda
	Grapefruit wedge, to garnish

In a big wineglass, combine the Aperol and Lillet ● If you like your drinks on the dry side, add the grapefruit bitters. If you prefer it a little more sweet, ditch the bitters entirely ● Add ice ● Top with the sparkling rosé, then club soda ● Garnish with the grapefruit wedge ●

CATHARSIS

A BREAKUP *Palate Cleanser*

Serves 1 Let's be clear: after getting this all out, I want to be as far from this event, and the people involved, as possible. This vodka spritz is topped with a scoop of sorbet, a traditional palate cleanser during a meal. Drink it to rid yourself of the bad taste in your mouth and move the fuck on, better and stronger.

2 oz.	vodka
6 to 7 oz.	prosecco
1 scoop	sorbet, flavor of your choice
	Lemon twist, to garnish (optional)

Add the vodka to a Champagne glass ●
Top with the prosecco, leaving enough room for the sorbet to fit in the glass ●
Add the sorbet, then garnish with the lemon twist, if desired ●

LEMONADE

WHEN LIFE GIVES you *Lemons*

Serves 1 This refreshing adult lemonade topped with basil is a tribute to Beyoncé's album *Lemonade,* which came out when she was dealing with betrayal and hardship in her own life. I listened to it on repeat as all of this happened to me, playing it at full volume and screaming the lyrics at the top of my lungs with my friends. I look at Beyoncé with such admiration because she figuratively took lemons and made lemonade, coming out the other side stronger and more resilient.

I wanted to be able to do that. It's usually in my nature to isolate, retreat, or disappear when things are hard. My friends told me I'd rise above this, but I didn't really believe them. I know Beyoncé's story is her story and mine is mine; this is my tribute to her, given with so much respect and appreciation. Drink this with your besties while blasting Queen Bey, baseball bat optional.

1½ oz.	vodka
½ oz.	gin
¾ oz.	fresh lemon juice
¾ oz.	simple syrup (page 170)
	Ice cubes
	Club soda, to top
	Fresh basil leaves, to garnish
	Lemon wheel, to garnish

Combine the vodka, gin, lemon juice, and syrup in a shaker tin with ice ● Shake to chill ● Strain into a Collins glass over fresh ice ● Top with the club soda, and garnish with the basil and lemon wheel ●

Dead WEIGHT

FOR LEAVING *the Worst Behind*

Serves 1 Right after the news of the affair broke, I went to Mexico for my friend's wedding, still in shock from it all. That first night I had a cathartic conversation with some of my oldest friends, and when I got back to my hotel room, my Los Angeles neighbor texted me and asked if I could keep the music down at the house. I realized my ex was having a party while I was out of town. My friend went by the house the next day to check on my dog and cat, and found my ex passed out on the couch, still in his clothes.

In that moment, something finally shifted in me. I decided I would no longer let his behavior get me down. I started to think about everything in a different way, like maybe it was the perfect time to start shedding dead weight. In this Dark and Stormy–inspired highball, I top with bitters and swap the traditional dark rum for light as we emerge from the wreckage.

2 oz.	light rum
¾ oz.	fresh lime juice
½ oz.	simple syrup (page 170)
	Ice cubes
	Ginger beer, to top
	Angostura bitters, to float

Shake the rum, lime juice, and syrup together in a shaker tin with ice ● Strain into a Collins glass over fresh ice cubes ● Top with the ginger beer ● Dash enough Angostura bitters over the drink so a thin line of bitters sits on top ●

No Saints, NO ANGELS

A BERRY *Frosé*

to brighten your day

1 bottle	Vanderpump rosé wine, in freezer overnight
2 cups	hulled and quartered fresh strawberries
2 cups	frozen raspberries
1 cup	Splenda (or your favorite sugar substitute)
1 cup	water
3 oz.	fresh lemon juice
	Ice cubes
	Mint sprigs, to garnish

Serves 4 Some people believe that if you're not an angel, or a saint, or a perfect person, then you almost deserve it when something horrible happens to you. I am the first one to say that I'm not a perfect person! But that does not mean that I deserve the kind of heartbreak my ex dished out. We're all just out here doing our best. Treat yourself to this blissed out Vanderpump frosé whenever you need to remind yourself that all we can do is work on ourselves, do our best, and leave the rest.

NOTE ● Regular simple syrup would work in this drink, but I like using a sugar substitute to keep the vibes even lighter.

Place the wine, strawberries, raspberries, sweetener, water, and lemon juice in a blender with 1 cup of ice cubes ● Blend on low, gradually increasing the speed as the ingredients start to turn into slush ● When completely smooth, pour into glasses ● Garnish with mint sprigs ●

REVENGE Dress

BEST *served cold*

Serves 1 Before the taping of the *Vanderpump Rules* reunion show, I got together with my amazing stylist Emily Men to figure out what to wear for the episode. For most reunion shows, I would wear something simple, like a little black dress, but I knew this time around my outfit needed to make a bold statement. When she pulled out an amazing red top and skirt combo, we were both immediately obsessed. During the taping, Andy Cohen mentioned how it reminded him of Princess Diana's iconic revenge dress after Prince Charles confessed his infidelity on national television. Turns out the best way to get revenge on an ex is to simply remind them of how you're a total firecracker, with or without them.

As a tribute to that bold red dress, this cocktail is a fiery red Negroni made with strawberry-infused Campari.

1 oz. Strawberry-Infused Campari (recipe follows)
1 oz. gin
1 oz. sweet vermouth
Ice cubes
Orange peel, to garnish

Combine the Campari, gin, and vermouth in a mixing glass with ice ● Stir to chill ● Strain into a rocks glass over several fresh ice cubes ● Garnish with an orange peel ●

STRAWBERRY-INFUSED CAMPARI

10 strawberries
12 oz. Campari aperitivo

Makes 12 ounces Cut the green tops off of the strawberries and cut them in half ● Combine with 12 ounces of Campari in a large jar with a lid ● Shake to combine ● Let the berries infuse overnight ● Strain the Campari into another jar ● (Keep the infused strawberries; they're delicious on their own or spooned over vanilla ice cream) ● Store the infusion in the jar for up to 30 days in the refrigerator ●

SELF-CARE

^A REVITALIZING *Aloe Elixir*

Serves 1 For me, self-care usually happens in three stages. The first is chain smoking and drinking too much rosé, probably because I am in a little bit of denial. The second is finding support from my friends. The third is taking care of myself in the best ways I know how—maybe getting a facial or massage, or hanging out with my dog on the couch in my pajamas, watching good reality television. In times that call for that kind of self-care, I like this low-proof tonic made with aloe liqueur. It tastes so soothing and revitalizing, and because there isn't a lot of alcohol involved, you can have a few with no regrets.

NOTE ● **Aloe liqueur is so cooling it almost tastes healthy. It's a great bottle to add to your home bar. I find it works really well with clear spirits like tequila and vodka. Add some to a margarita or serve simply with soda (like in this drink) or even sparkling wine for an effortless weeknight highball.**

2	cucumber slices, peeled and quartered, to muddle
2 oz.	Chareau aloe liqueur (see Note)
	Ice cubes
	Club soda, to top
	Mint bouquet, to garnish

In a Collins glass, muddle the cucumber slices together with the liqueur ● Add the ice, then top with the club soda ● Garnish with the mint bouquet ●

Self-Care

Cold
SHOULDER

An ARCTIC *hit of mint*

Serves 1 This ice-cold shot made with frosty crème de menthe represents the times when it's necessary to give the people who have betrayed you the cold shoulder. One of the hardest things about getting through the aftermath of a breakup like this is finding a way to exist in the same spaces as my ex and ex-friend—we all had to be present to film the reunion episodes, we're all mentioned in the same stories, and for a while, he and I were still living in the same house as we figured out how to deal with the logistics of our breakup. The media was constantly asking me what I thought about the things they were saying and the way they behaved. I am moving forward with my life, and they can move forward with theirs too.

NOTE ● Make sure you shake this shot long and hard—until the shaker tin feels so cold you might drop it—so that when you shoot it, the boozy mix sends shivers down your spine.

1 sprig	mint, to muddle
½ oz.	crème de menthe
½ oz.	vodka
	Ice cubes

In a shaker tin, muddle the mint sprig ● Add the créme de menthe and vodka ● Shake hard with ice to chill (see Note) ● Strain into a shot glass ● To make more than one, simply multiply the quantities ●

In the SPOTLIGHT

A SASSY *Peach-tini*

Serves 1 Part of being on a reality TV show is trying to find some level of peace with always being in the spotlight. Since we started our relationship on the show, every little detail was scrutinized for the entire nine years we were together, so I had sort of gotten used to the attention. But when the news of the affair broke, things catapulted to a totally new level. Seeing #Scandoval trending on social media and watching so many dedicated fans rally behind me as #TeamAriana is truly surreal. At times, it has even been overwhelming to read everybody's comments—both positive and negative—but I read and replied to a lot of them anyway because I want people to know that I do pay attention, and I appreciate all the signs of support.

Next time you're enjoying your favorite reality TV show, whip up a sassy drink like this one that bursts with bright citrus and fresh peaches.

½	peach, peeled and pitted
½ oz.	simple syrup (page 170)
2 oz.	vodka
¾ oz.	fresh lemon juice
¼ oz.	Cointreau liqueur
	Ice cubes
	Lemon twist, to garnish

Muddle the peach in the bottom of a shaker tin with the simple syrup ● Add the vodka, lemon juice, and Cointreau, plus ice ● Shake to chill ● Strain into a martini glass, and garnish with a lemon twist ●

Ride–OR-DIE

ᴬ REFRESHING
Mezcal Paloma

Serves 1 From the very beginning of our relationship, I prided myself on being his ride-or-die. Whatever I was going through, whatever he was going through—he was my end game, my life partner. I am the kind of person who will always be there for my partner. That quality may have left me vulnerable in this case, but it's something I don't want to lose in myself in the future, despite the devastation I've experienced. If I were to lose that all-in part of my identity, it would make me a lesser version of myself.

A good mezcal paloma is one of my ride-or-die cocktails— so easy to make and always reliably delicious. Drink it knowing that you can put this all behind you, and there will be others deserving of your loyalty and love.

2 oz.	mezcal
1 oz.	fresh grapefruit juice
¾ oz.	fresh lime juice
½ oz.	agave nectar
1 to 2 dashes	chili bitters
	Ice cubes
	Grapefruit soda, to top
1	grapefruit wedge, to garnish

Combine the mezcal, citrus juices, agave nectar, and chili bitters in a shaker tin with ice and shake to chill ● Strain into a Collins glass over fresh ice ● Top with the grapefruit soda, then garnish with a grapefruit wedge ●

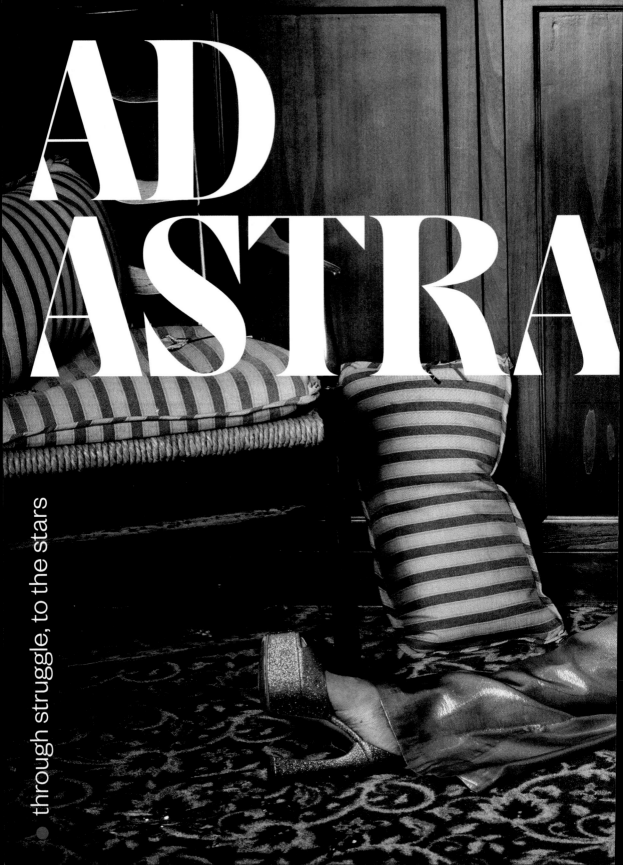

AD ASTRA

through struggle, to the stars

what, Doesn't KILL ME

COURAGE via *Chartreuse*

Serves 1 Music helps me in so many ways, and "what doesn't kill me better run" is a favorite lyric from Kacey Musgraves, who I'm a big fan of. That mentality shoved me forward during the hardest times. In the face of betrayal and depression, anxiety, loss, and grief, instead of retreating, I'm stepping up and drawing the battle lines. Not backing down. What doesn't kill me better get out of my way.

When I think about a big dose of liquid courage, yellow Chartreuse always comes to mind. It is a high-proof, herbaceous liqueur that can taste polarizing to some people, but I love the way it promises a honeyed sweetness in addition to a big punch of booze.

2 oz.	brandy
¾ oz.	Yellow Chartreuse liqueur
¾ oz.	fresh lemon juice
½ oz.	canned pineapple juice
¼ oz.	simple syrup (page 170)
	Crushed ice
	Mint bouquet, to garnish

Combine the brandy, Chartreuse, lemon juice, pineapple juice, and syrup in a Collins glass ● Add crushed ice ● Swizzle using a bar spoon ● Top with more crushed ice, so it reaches the top of the glass ● Garnish with the mint bouquet ●

GRATITUDE

FRESH and *uplifting*

2	mint sprigs
½ oz.	honey syrup (page 170)
2 oz.	white rum
¾ oz.	fresh lime juice
¾ oz.	St-Germain elderflower liqueur
	Ice cubes

Serves 1 I wish I had the words to properly express the gratitude I have for my friends, family, and supporters—not just during this tough time but others too. Whenever I am struggling, and it's hard for me to ask for help, I have friends and family who always show up for me. When my light is dimmed, my friends ignite my confidence to help me shine. I hope that throughout my life I am able to give that back to those people.

I can only show gratitude through my actions and in being the best friend I can be to those who were there for me. These are my flowers for those people, a subtly fresh floral cocktail made with St-Germain. It's a toast to everyone who has ever been there for me when times got hard.

Muddle the mint and syrup together in a shaker tin ● Add the rum, lime juice, and liqueur and shake with ice to chill ● Strain into a coupe glass ●

Oaxacan FLAME

AN OLD FASHIONED for *New Beginnings*

Serves 1 A few weeks after I found out about the affair, I traveled to Oaxaca, Mexico, for a friend's wedding, and that is when the first mental shift away from all the horrible feelings began. I was there with a very old friend group—some of them have known me for twenty years, when I was fresh out of college. The conversations we had really helped me connect back to that person I used to be, before any of this stuff happened. They knew the true me.

While I was there, I met a really lovely, incredible man. We stayed up the entire night after the wedding just getting to know each other, talking about our families, dreams, and goals. It felt like divine intervention, the way he appeared during one of my darkest moments. He respected my request that nothing would happen beyond talking that night. He was excited to just spend more time together, getting to know the real me. That gave me the biggest feeling of hope for my future.

It's time to say goodbye to old flames and welcome the new. This is not the end; it's just the beginning.

NOTE ● Flex your bartending skills by flaming an orange peel. Here's how you do it: Using an abundance of caution, hold the peel about an inch above the cocktail, with the skin side facing the drink. Light a match and hold it underneath the skin. Quickly and forcefully, squeeze the peel to press the oils into the flame.

2 oz.	mezcal
½ oz.	Nixta Licor de Elote
¼ oz.	agave nectar
1 dash	chocolate bitters
	Ice cubes, including 1 large ice cube for serving
	Orange peel, to garnish

Combine the mezcal, liqueur, agave nectar, and bitters in a mixing glass with ice ● Stir to chill ● Strain into a rocks glass over 1 large ice cube ● To garnish, flame the orange peel over the drink (see Note) ● Garnish with the peel ●

Karma Is My BOYFRIEND

SWEET **like** *honey*

Serves 1   A lot of people believe that karma is a cosmic force that either rewards or punishes you for good or bad deeds. Though some have said this affair was bad karma coming to get me, I don't see it that way. I think the universe shoved me in a different direction because I wasn't where I was supposed to be. So many amazing things have come from this trial by fire, and I'm emerging from it stronger than before.

The name of this cocktail is from a lyric in one of my favorite Taylor Swift songs. It's a perfect representation for dancing into your power—making karma not your enemy but your boyfriend.

2 oz.	gin
¾ oz.	fresh lemon juice
¾ oz.	honey syrup (page 170)
¼ oz.	Licor 43 vanilla liqueur
	Ice cubes
3 drops	Angostura bitters, to garnish

Combine the gin, lemon juice, syrup, and liqueur in a shaker tin with ice and shake to chill ● Strain into a coupe glass ● To garnish, place three drops of bitters across the top of the drink ●

THR

Sometimes the media paints singles as desperate and lonely, but there is so much power to be found in being your own best partner. Here are ten reasons you can enjoy being single and you'll find yourself thriving, not just surviving: • Time to focus on your own growth and self-worth • No more choosing between families during the holidays •

Having the bandwidth to prioritize your career, if you want ● Spontaneity! You don't have to run every decision by your SO ● 100 percent of your social attention can go toward your friendships ● It's more fun to flirt with no strings attached ● The house can stay as clean—or as messy—as you desire ● You get to pick what to watch for movie night. Every night ●

NEW YORK

A SWEET *Cherry Kiss*

Serves 1 I lived in New York City before I moved to Los Angeles, but for this drink, I am using New York as a metaphor for the wonderful person I met in Oaxaca after I broke up with my ex. New York is the most amazing person, one who has lifted me up on so many levels—friendship, spiritual, and romantic. When I'm with him, I never feel more seen, more heard, more myself. I can finally relax. There's excitement and happiness, but nothing about it feels jealous, insecure, or scared. It truly feels like I was made for New York and New York was made for me.

When this book comes out, if we don't end up together, that's totally fine, too. The growth, love, and support I have felt during this difficult time make everything worth it. I have found a true gem amid the chaos, and this New York sour made with sweet cherries is dedicated to him.

NOTE ● I like the texture that the egg white (or vegan aquafaba, page 171) supplies, but if it's not for you, feel free to skip it.

5	sweet cherries, pitted
2 oz.	high-proof rye whiskey
¾ oz.	fresh lemon juice
¾ oz.	simple syrup (page 170)
1	egg white or 1 oz. aquafaba (optional, see Note)
	Ice cubes, including 1 large ice cube for serving
1 oz.	dry red wine, to float

Muddle the cherries in the bottom of the shaker tin ● Add the rye whiskey, lemon juice, simple syrup, and egg white (if using) ● Shake to combine ● Add ice and shake again to chill ● Strain into a rocks glass over 1 large ice cube ● Float the red wine over the top ●

BREAD-WINNER

POUR MYSELF
a cup of *ambition*

Serves 1 During the aftermath of this breakup, I feel grateful that I've been given some really incredible opportunities to move on to a new level of independence as a woman. I've had the chance to really look myself in the mirror and realize I am the breadwinner—and I always have been. I deserve good things but I didn't see that in myself for so long.

The name of this cocktail takes inspiration from two of the most badass women in country music, Dolly Parton and Kacey Musgraves. It is a sparkly, smoky twist on the Gold Rush cocktail, made with Scotch and edible gold flakes, because I'm earning what's mine and I'm not going to apologize for it.

1½ oz.	whiskey
½ oz.	Scotch whiskey
¾ oz.	fresh lemon juice
¾ oz.	honey syrup (page 170)
	Ice cubes
	Edible gold flakes, to garnish

Combine the whiskeys, lemon juice, and syrup in a shaker tin with ice and shake to chill ● Strain into a rocks glass over fresh ice ● Garnish with a sprinkle of the edible gold flakes ●

MY LAST Word

DOING It
My Way

¾ oz.	tequila
¾ oz.	fresh lime juice
¾ oz.	Green Chartreuse liqueur
¾ oz.	maraschino liqueur
	Ice cubes
1	Luxardo maraschino cherry, to garnish
	Lime peel, to garnish

Serves 1 My ex is one of those men who was always determined to have the last word in every argument. He'd be so upset if I didn't admit I was wrong, even when I knew I was right. This cocktail is a riff on the classic Last Word cocktail because this time I have the last word. Made with tequila instead of gin, I love how in my take, the Chartreuse has a cool herbaceous quality that pairs well with the agave spirit.

In a shaker tin, add the tequila, lime juice, Chartreuse, and maraschino liqueur ● Shake with ice, then strain into the glass ● To garnish, skewer the maraschino cherry and lime peel on a cocktail pick ●

COVER GIRL

LEMON DROP *mic drop*

Serves 1 In early June 2023, I landed my first cover story for *Glamour* magazine. They called it "The Vindication of Ariana Madix," which was a nice surprise. I love how the article came together with the help of a bunch of talented women—Sylvia Wheeler put my hair in a nice simple bun, Diana de Silva made my skin glow with a very stripped-down look, and the photographer, Celeste Sloman, made the whole thing feel effortless. For the photos, my stylist Emily Men was so clever to take the opposite of the Revenge Dress look by having me wear jeans and a simple white tank top. A lot of people loved how breezy the whole thing felt, which reminded me that a good mic drop doesn't always have to be in-your-face; sometimes it's just living your best life.

In the spirit of laid-back, effortless power, this is a grown-up version of the lemon drop shot—the subtly sweet apricot balances out the sour pucker.

2 oz.	vodka
¾ oz.	lemon juice
¾ oz.	apricot liqueur
½ oz.	simple syrup (page 170)
	ice cubes

Combine the vodka, lemon juice, apricot liqueur, and simple syrup in a shaker tin with ice and shake to chill ● Strain into a martini glass ● Just like its namesake shot, don't let this cocktail sit around— drink it quickly while still ice cold! ●

Life Is BEAUTIFUL

A BREATH of *fresh air*

Serves 1 Looking back on all this—the last months of chaos, nine years we spent together, thirty-eight years of my life—there have been some really low lows, some really high highs, and so many moments in between. Every day, I try to remember all the ways I am blessed, beyond the chaos and bad things that happen. I take inventory and remember the wonderful people who love me. Just sitting with my dog and cat and hanging out, or going for a walk and feeling the breeze on my cheeks—these small acts are forms of daily gratitude.

They remind me that I don't need to cling to everything that existed in my life before, because sometimes what is coming next is so much better. This drink features a delicious alcohol-free replacement for gin, plus rosemary syrup— together they remind me of taking a walk in a garden, soaking in all of life's beautiful moments.

2 oz.	Seedlip Garden 108
¾ oz.	fresh lemon juice
¾ oz.	rosemary syrup (page 171)
	Ice cubes
	Alcohol-free sparkling wine, to top
	Fresh rosemary sprig, to garnish
	Lemon wheel, to garnish

In a shaker tin, combine the Seedlip with the lemon juice and rosemary syrup ● Add ice and shake to chill ● Strain into a wineglass ● Top with the sparkling wine ● Garnish with a rosemary sprig and lemon wheel ●

We Ride at AT DAWN

EQUAL PARTS
Power **and** *Healing*

	Lime wedge, to rim the glass
	Kosher salt, to rim the glass
2 oz.	mezcal
¾ oz.	fresh lime juice
¾ oz.	rosemary syrup (page 171)
	Ice cubes
	Rosemary sprig, to garnish

Serves 1 Mezcal margaritas are among my favorite drinks—big, bold, and powerful.

I've talked to so many people who have gone through a horrible breakup like this. Everyone wants to be in love, and it's so easy to lose yourself in a relationship. I did, and I didn't even realize it at the time.

This cocktail is a battle cry for anyone who might be going through similar tough times. When we feel like we're wavering, we need to gather our strength and hold fast. We can accomplish so much when we own our power. Let's ride away from the negativity and pain, and remember we are badass, beautiful human beings—and nobody can take that away from us.

Prepare your rocks glass by running a lime wedge along the rim of half the glass and dipping the rim in salt ● Combine the mezcal, lime juice, and syrup in a shaker tin with ice and shake to chill ● Add fresh ice to the glass, then strain the cocktail into it ● To garnish, light the tip of the rosemary sprig on fire—once it has extinguished and is smoking slightly, place inside the glass ● Wait until the smoke has dissipated fully to serve ●

BASICS

Making syrups at home is a quick and easy endeavor. Most of the time, all you need is water, sugar, and whatever ingredients you are using to flavor the syrup. Most bartenders use plain white sugar because its flavor is neutral, but you can use raw sugar or your favorite sugar substitute (like Splenda) if you prefer.

If you are feeling lazy, some of these syrups are also available for sale in grocery stores and online; for example, I really like the richness of the grenadine from Liber & Co., and they have a chai syrup that would make for a great alternative to the black tea syrup, too. You could use regular orgeat instead of the DIY version on page 171 (Small Hand Foods makes a gourmet one), and I have also seen aquafaba powder for sale at grocery stores like Whole Foods, which you just have to add water to, if you don't want to deal with a whole can of chickpeas.●

Simple Syrup

Simple syrup is the easiest syrup to make and the most versatile one you can have in your cocktail repertoire. If you don't want to use real sugar, that's okay—you can use your sugar substitute of choice.

Makes about 1½ cups
1 cup sugar
1 cup water

In a small saucepan, combine the sugar and water. Slowly bring to a boil over medium heat, stirring to make sure the sugar doesn't burn. Remove from the heat when the sugar is fully dissolved. Allow to cool. Store in a bottle in the refrigerator for up to a few weeks.

Honey Syrup

I absolutely adore the way honey tastes in cocktails. Its warmth adds something special in a way that white sugar or stevia can't replicate. Honey syrup is also fun because you can customize the flavor based on the type of honey you use. Regular honey works fine, but I also like orange blossom honey for extra floral notes, or manuka honey, which has a caramelized quality to it.

Makes about 1½ cups
1 cup honey
1 cup water

Combine the honey and water in a mason jar and shake to combine. Store in a bottle in the refrigerator for up to a few weeks.

Grenadine

There are plenty of delicious commercial grenadines you can buy at the store, but it's also an ingredient you can whip up in a snap at home.

Makes about 1½ cups
1 cup POM pomegranate juice
1 cup sugar
1 teaspoon orange blossom water (optional)

Combine the ingredients in a mason jar or other container with a lid. Shake to combine. (If you prefer your grenadine to have a more caramelized flavor, you can heat the ingredients up in a saucepan on the stove like you would with a simple syrup. Remove from heat after it comes to a boil, then stir until the sugar is dissolved.) Store in a bottle in the refrigerator for up to a few weeks.

Black Tea Syrup

This is a super versatile recipe because you can use any kind of tea. The Gaslight cocktail (page 102) tastes great with a black tea like Earl Grey or English Breakfast.

Makes about 1½ cups
1 cup sugar
1 cup water
2 black tea bags

In a small saucepan, bring the sugar and water to a boil over medium heat, stirring so the sugar doesn't burn the bottom of the pan. Remove from heat once the sugar is dissolved. Add tea bags and let steep for 3 minutes. Remove tea bags. Store in a bottle in the refrigerator for up to a few weeks.

Vanilla Syrup

Vanilla syrup tastes great with aged spirits like whiskey and rum. I always recommend using real vanilla beans to get the best flavor—vanilla extract will get the job done but will taste a little lackluster in comparison.

Makes about 1½ cups

1 cup sugar
1 cup water
½ teaspoon vanilla extract

In a small saucepan, bring the sugar and water to a boil over medium heat, stirring so the sugar doesn't burn the bottom of the pan. Remove from heat once the sugar is dissolved. Stir in the vanilla extract. Let cool. Store the syrup in a bottle in the refrigerator for up to a few weeks.

Sunflower Orgeat Syrup

Orgeat is a nut-based syrup commonly used in tropical cocktails. I like to use sunflower seeds instead of almonds because the seeds require less water to grow so they are the more sustainable option. You could use any nut here, but I like the way the sunflowers taste alongside the passion fruit in the Support System cocktail (page 118).

Makes about 2 cups

1 cup sunflower seeds, unsalted
1½ cups water
1 cup sugar

In a small saucepan, toast the sunflowers over medium heat, stirring frequently, until they become fragrant. Remove from heat. Combine the water, sugar, and sunflower seeds in a blender and process until smooth. Store in the refrigerator for up to 2 weeks.

Rosemary Syrup

Fresh herbs are a great way to add a subtle savory or herbaceous note to cocktails. I especially like rosemary together with gin or vodka. This recipe can also be adapted for other kinds of herbs, like lavender or thyme—or both! Just swap in 2 sprigs of your herb of choice for the rosemary in this recipe.

Makes about 1½ cups

1 cup sugar
1 cup water
2 sprigs fresh rosemary

Combine the sugar and water in a small saucepan. Slowly bring to a boil over medium heat, stirring so the sugar doesn't stick to the bottom of the pan. Remove from the heat once the sugar is dissolved. Add the herb sprigs and stir to combine. Let sit for 10 minutes and taste. If the herb flavor is strong enough for your liking, remove the sprigs and allow the syrup to fully cool. If it's not stong enough, let steep for 5 more minutes. Store in a bottle in the refrigerator for up to a few weeks.

Aquafaba

Egg whites add a great fluffy texture to cocktails, but for some people the idea of adding raw eggs to a drink is off-putting. Aquafaba is a great substitute—it brings the same frothy goodness to a drink but without adding any flavor. It's the liquid from a can of chickpeas, so it's also a fantastic option for vegetarians and vegans who want to avoid using animal products in their drinks.

Makes about 2 cups

1 (15-ounce) can chickpeas

Drain a can of chickpeas, reserving the liquid. (Save the beans for some other use.) In a medium bowl, whip the liquid with a hand mixer or stand mixer until the texture becomes close to whipped cream. You can do this with a whisk, too, but it will take a lot more elbow grease and more time to get the right consistency. Store in an airtight container in the refrigerator for up to 1 week.

THANKS

to Meredith Brace Sloss for rallying the Madix Support Team when I needed it the most, and to all of those friends who showed up and helped keep my spirits lifted, including: Logan Cochran, Scheana Shay, Simon Curtis, Dayna Kathan, Brad Kearns, Kristen Doute, Katie Maloney, Janet Caperna, Jared Lipscomb, Courtney Berman, Lindsay Elizabeth Hand, Jean Luis Fragnay, Krystina Arielle, Raleigh Seldon, Megan Rooney, Lucinda Pace, Carla Furey, and Ali Rafiq (who has since passed; our brisket text group misses you!).

To my agent David Doerrer, manager Kasra Ajir, and assistant Lauren Davis for getting this project together and for helping keep the schedule on track.

To the whole Clarkson Potter team for making this book a reality: Jennifer Sit, Bianca Cruz, Mark McCauslin, Laura Palese, Stephanie Huntwork, Phil Leung, Allison Renzulli, Chloe Aryeh, Erica Gelbard, and Jana Branson.

To Emma Janzen, my partner in crime in words and drinks.

To the incredible photo team led by Kelly Puleio, including Tamara Costa, Katja Bresch, Trevin Hutchins, Lena Conley, Maxwell Newton, Cory Fisher, Brandon Loyd, and Wendy Helie. Special thanks to Scottie Harvey, along with Studio 3XP, Hot Set Props, and Brute Botanical.

To my stylist, Emily Men, who, as always, nailed every outfit, and to my hair stylist, Bradley Leake, and makeup stylist, Diane da Silva.

To the brands who contributed to the looks throughout the book: Abercrombie & Fitch, Acler, Alo, Betsey Johnson, Boys Lie, Calzedonia, AKNVAS, Charles & Keith, commando, Dynamite, Elle Zeitoune Designs, FWRD, Granny Men's Jewelry, Jenny Bird, Jessica Simpson Collection, KBH Jewels, Ksubi, Monique Lhuillier, Nasty Gal, Needle & Thread, Nina Shoes, Rebecca Minkoff, REVOLVE, Romwe, Saint Haven, Sam Edelman, Shay Jewelry, ShopBop, Steve Madden, and The Sei.

To my mom, Tanya Madix, and brother, Jeremy Madix, for their unconditional love and support.

To my ex, for showing me that I could learn to love myself outside of any type of relationship. I wish him the best.

Index